TEDDY BEARS

A History and Collector's Guide

Lorraine Hitchings

AMBERLEY

First published 2018

Amberley Publishing
The Hill, Stroud
Gloucestershire, GL5 4EP

www.amberley-books.com

Copyright © Lorraine Hitchings, 2018

The right of Lorraine Hitchings to be identified
as the Author of this work has been asserted in
accordance with the Copyrights, Designs and
Patents Act 1988.

ISBN 978 1 4456 8049 1 (print)
ISBN 978 1 4456 8050 7 (ebook)

British Library Cataloguing in Publication Data.
A catalogue record for this book is available from
the British Library.

Origination by Amberley Publishing.
Printed in the UK.

Contents

Introduction

Teddy Bear; for the vast majority of us, these two words conjure up a picture in our minds of a soft toy from our childhood whose eyes are a bit wobbly, whose nose has probably almost disappeared, whose fur has all been loved off and who is possibly missing an ear. He may very well be stored away somewhere along with all the memories you once shared, but you have never forgotten him – you never could. If he has been one of those lucky bears, he might still be sitting upon your bed, just as he did when you were a child. It is because of all the wear he has and because of all the hands that have held him that he seems to have a special warmth and ability to evoke the past. The teddy bear may bring wonderful memories of childhood flooding back to our minds, and maybe it is because of this that we love him so much, but I would argue that the teddy bear is something more than memories; I believe he is something rather special, rather unique and rather outstanding.

This old teddy bear from the 1930s, known as Floppy-Ross, is a typical idea of a teddy from our childhood.

Beginnings

The teddy bear is absolutely brimming over with myths and legends, many of them being tied up with his origins, and although it feels as if he has been in our lives forever, he hasn't actually been around as long as you might think.

The way he came into our lives is also rather curious. To tell you the full story, we need to go back in time to a small town in Giengen, Germany, and to the year 1847, when a little girl named Apollonia Margarete Steiff was born on 24 July. For the first eighteen months of her life she was a healthy child, but she then contracted polio, which left her with a weakened right arm, a paralysed left foot and a partially paralysed right foot. After travelling the length and breadth of Germany to find a cure for the young Margarete, her parents soon realised that their daughter would be confined to a wheelchair for the rest of her life. Nevertheless, apart from her disabilities, Margarete was an extremely bright and loving child who everyone adored, but on leaving school in 1861, she had a very uncertain future ahead of her, as the only thing she could do was sew. Deciding to be a seamstress, she found sewing for long hours was difficult, and so she bought herself a sewing machine, which was probably the very first in Giengen. This was not without its problems, as Margarete found it difficult to turn the wheel of the machine with her right hand and so she turned the sewing machine around and taught herself to turn the wheel with her left hand. She attended sewing school to learn the trade and also to perfect her sewing skills. Her work proved to be very good and friends persuaded her to start her own business. In 1877 she started the Felt Store and soon was employing a number of local women to help produce some fine felt garments. Margarete found it impossible to attend trade shows and so she bought fashion magazines that would help her keep up to date with the latest styles. One of those magazines was called *Modenwelt* and it was in this magazine that she discovered a pattern for a tiny elephant pincushion. Margarete was intrigued by the pattern and decided to use some of the felt off-cuts she had lying around the workshop to make one. Pleased with the result, she made a couple and gave them away to family and friends. Everyone loved them, especially the children. You see, in those times children only had very hard toys to play with that were made from wood, or even metal. Even dolls were made of hard materials, so when Margarete's little felt elephants made an appearance, it is no wonder they were loved so much. Requests for more and more elephants came in and on 29 December 1880 Margarete began to put them into production. In 1885 some 600 elephants were produced and one year later the figure increased to 5,000. The company flourished and soon more felt animals were added to the company's catalogue. In 1889, the company moved to larger premises and in 1892 it applied for a patent for making animals and other figures. It was during this same

Two old Steiff bears named Smokey (the larger one) and Polly.

Margarete Steiff, who spent most of her life in a wheelchair after contracting polio in 1849. (Image courtesy of Steiff GmbH)

year that the company made its first bear, which was, unusually, for a skittles set. What the company noticed was that the bear from that skittles set was often removed from the set and played with as a single toy. So was this to be the start of the Steiff Bear? Margarete Steiff soon discovered that she needed some help in running the expanding company and for this she turned to her brother Fritz and his sons, Richard, Franz, Paul, Otto, Hugo and Ernst.

Richard Steiff

Born on 7 February 1877, the second son of Fritz Steiff and his wife Anna, Richard was the first of Margarete's nephews to join her company. It was always believed that he was her favourite nephew as he always seemed to capture his aunt's attention. Richard was sent to the Commercial Art School in Stuttgart by his father, a leading mason, and upon leaving college he joined his aunt's company. His first proper job was to represent the company at the Leipzig Trade Festival and he was later sent to England, where he became popular with both customers and his fellow businessmen. Upon his return to Germany, he spent many hours talking to his aunt about the business and it was agreed that the company needed some new ideas. During the late nineteenth century, Richard designed many soft toys, among them a Bear-On-Wheels. These bears proved popular and he also produced some bears that were not on wheels, that stood upright on

Richard Steiff, father of the teddy bear. (Image courtesy of Steiff GmbH)

their hind legs; but what he did notice was that these bears still could not be cuddled. Children needed a toy that they could hold close, not a toy with a metal frame that made them hard to touch. In 1902, when the first street lanterns were being installed in cities and the Wright brothers were making their first attempts at taking to the skies, something new and very important happened in the toy world. Richard designed a bear that was moveable due to a series of string joints; a bear that could be held in a child's arms and hugged. These bears met with a cool response by his aunt; not one to give up easily, Richard finally produced a bear that his aunt liked and accepted for production. This was not the end of the story, however, because in March of 1903 the bear was taken to the Leipzig Toy Festival and was received with a very cold response; he was even referred to as a 'stuffed misfit.' Disheartened, Richard packed his bears away. But then something else happened and the course of history was to be changed forever when a man named Hermann Berg (who was the chief buyer for a New York wholesaler George Borgfeldt & Co.) came to the Steiff stand. He told Richard he was looking for new ideas at the festival but had found nothing. Pulling out one of his bears and putting it into Berg's hands, an order for 3,000 was immediately placed and the rest, as they say, is history. That is until the bear got his name, because you see at this time he was still not called Teddy.

The Roosevelt Connection

As previously mentioned, the teddy bear is surrounded by tons of myths and legends, possibly because he has become an international star! His story is a magical one indeed, which even has connections with the United States and one of the country's ex-presidents. So to begin this part of his story, let us return to the year 1902 (the year Richard Steiff created the first bear), but this time let us travel to the southern United States, to the Louisiana and Mississippi border, where President Theodore Roosevelt (known as Teddy to his friends) found himself called to settle a dispute over a frontier. In order to gain the President's favour while there, he was invited to a bear hunt. The President was well known for his love of hunting and sadly, during those times, both animal welfare and ecology were of little concern; bears were simply seen as vicious predators and so were legitimate targets for hunters. On the day of the hunt, however, not a single bear could be found. The President's hosts were somewhat embarrassed by this and felt they had to provide the President with a trophy to take home so they came up with the idea of capturing an old and infirm bear, tying him to a stake and then calling the President to shoot it. Roosevelt, when hearing the commotion outside his tent, found himself almost face to face with the sad old bear. Having no taste for such a victory, he viewed his hosts with great contempt, saying, 'If I killed this bear I could never look my children in the eye again.' Meanwhile, witnessing the entire event was the political cartoonist Clifford Berryman, who made a sketch of the whole affair and later published it in the *Washington Post*, naming the cartoon 'Drawing the Line in Mississippi.' It is worth remembering that teddy bears have been made and are sometimes still made with the famous face of that bear in Berryman's cartoon, commonly known as a Heart-Shaped Bear.

Now let us take our story back to a small shop in Brooklyn that was owned by Russian immigrants Morris and Rose Michtom. Always on the look-out for products to add to his shop window, Morris noticed the cartoon and asked his wife if she could produce a bear that looked like the one in the cartoon. She did and he put the bear in the window next to a copy of Berryman's cartoon. The bear sold quickly and Rose made more. They named it Teddy's Bear and so it is said that the Teddy Bear was born. Being a rather shrewd businessman, Michtom realised that he had to capitalise on his new idea and decided to name it after the President. It is said that he sent one of these bears to the White House with a note attached requesting he use the President's name, Teddy, and it is also said that a letter came back from the President saying, 'I don't believe that my name will do much for the image of your stuffed bear, but you have my permission to use it.' However, no proof of these letters have ever been found. He began selling vast amounts of his new idea, and as sales grew he decided to sell his new idea to one of America's largest toy makers, the Ideal Toy Corporation. When Michtom died in 1938, the White House sent a letter of condolence to his family.

Steiff's 'Roosevelt Bear', with a heart-shaped face taken from the cartoon bear made famous by Clifford Berryman.

His Journey

The wildfire popularity of the teddy bear spread across both sides of the Atlantic while, back in Germany, many soft toy companies began to market their versions of the teddy bear. Most companies copied those of his creators, Steiff, to the point of even putting buttons in their teddy bears' ears (a patent used by Steiff since 1904); that is, until Steiff took companies to court to stop them using it. In the United States the teddy epidemic really broke out in about 1906 and many toy companies started making their versions of the teddy, including a company called Bruin Manufacturing Company (BMC) that was established as early as 1907, based in New York City. Their bears resembled those of the Ideal Company. Other companies included the Aetna Toy Animal Company, which began in 1906 but lasted only a couple of years, the Columbia Teddy Bear Manufacturers, who used the name of the explorer Christopher Columbus to emphasise its Americanness, and the Strauss Manufacturing Co. Inc. (who advertised themselves as 'Toy King of New York'), to name but a few.

As far as Britain was concerned, it dragged its heels, saying that the teddy bear was simply a fad. However, there was one company, named Farnell, who did start making teddy bears; a company who has had a big impact on the history of the teddy bear, especially in Britain, not least because they were the creators of the famous Winnie-the-Pooh. The teddy bear is said to have first appeared in J. K. Farnell's catalogue in 1906 but as this cannot be substantiated with a copy of that catalogue, we cannot be sure of the date the first teddy was made in Britain; thanks to the London store of Harrods, however, we do know for certain that Farnell were producing teddy bears in 1910.

The teddy bear quickly became a part of our everyday life, not just as a child's toy but as a companion or lucky mascot to adults too. Take for example the ill-fated ship *Titanic*. I have often wondered how many teddy bears travelled on board. I do know of one, a little teddy bear made by the German makers Bing around 1904. This little bear was travelling with the Restaurant Manager, Gaspare 'Luigi' Gatti. The teddy was given to Gatti by his son Vittorio just before he boarded the ill-fated ship. Sadly, Gatti was one of the poor souls who did not survive the sinking and it is reported that he was last seen standing on the ship's deck, dressed very smartly in his uniform, with a blanket draped over his arm. His body was recovered and buried in Fairview Cemetery, Halifax, Nova Scotia, and the little bear, who was later discovered tucked safely inside his tobacco pouch in the top pocket of his coat, was later reunited with Gatti's widow, Vera. For a while the little bear was resident in a Museum of Childhood in Ribchester, where I was lucky enough to meet him. When the museum closed the little bear was sold at auction, I believe to a private collector for the sum of £9,500. The company Merrythought produced a replica of this little bear, who came complete with a presentation box that told his story.

An early American-made teddy bear named Mississippi, who lost an eye sometime in the past.

Bodhi, an early Farnell teddy bear. This company produced the first English-made teddy bear.

The Merrythought *Titanic* bear, complete with
a presentation box that tells the story of the little
bear owned by Luigi Gatti.

For collectors interested in *Titanic* history, I would also mention that this is not the only teddy bear who has connections with the *Titanic* tragedy. When news of the disaster broke, the whole of England went into mourning and many stores, including Harrods, dressed their windows as a mark of respect. Harrods wanted to use black teddy bears for this and Steiff was approached and asked just a few weeks after the disaster if they could produce some bears for this purpose. In response, they then produced their so-called 'Mourning Bears.' In total some 494 bears were made for the English market and out of these just twelve were centre-seamed. Margarete Steiff, being a very frugal woman, noticed that a lot of expensive mohair was being wasted when the teddy bears' heads were being cut from fabric, and so it was decided that every seventh bear or so that was cut, would have its head cut from two pieces of mohair and stitched down the centre. The fact that these bears were much fewer in number makes them much more desirable to collectors today.

Steiff requested enough mohair to produce 600 bears, some of which were intended for other markets. These black Mourning Bears again have many myths and legends attached to them, one of the tales being that the red felt placed behind their eyes represents red eyes due to tears. However, I have never been able to verify this with their makers and I believe it is there simply to show up their black eyes against their black mohair.

The teddy bear had by now made his way into the hearts of everyone who met him, and he had also started to earn his keep in the field of advertising. He could be seen everywhere, advertising biscuits, confectionery and much more. He was also being used on early postcards, which were fast becoming very popular as everyone loved him.

A Steiff black bear.

Teddy bears were often featured on postcards during the early years. This card is postmarked 1910.

An early postcard, postmarked 1917.

Above left: A Birthday Wishes card, postmarked 1920.

Above right: An early teddy bear Christmas card.

Then something terrible happened; the First World War began and with it came bans on all imports from Germany, and that sadly included the teddy bear. Back in Germany, factories were needed for important war work, including the Steiff factory, which was used to make felt uniforms for the Kaiser's army. Paul, Hugo, Otto and Richard were all young men and were called to do their duty; who knows, maybe they even wore uniforms that had been made in their own factory.

An often intimate and heart-breaking side of this war was the good luck charms that were carried by soldiers on both sides. Many carried crosses, items of broken jewellery, handkerchiefs and teddy bears, the hope being that these lucky talismans would bring them home safely. Many soldiers, we know, took their childhood teddy bears with them and many soft toy companies took advantage of this situation and began producing small teddy bears that would measure no more than a couple of inches that could be easily carried by soldiers. These little bears are now commonly known as 'Soldier Bears' or 'Sweetheart Bears.' They were given to soldiers by a loved one before leaving to fight abroad, hence their name. The British company Farnell was one of the companies who made these little bears, which were small enough to fit into a soldier's breast pocket, and whose eyes were sewn very high upon their heads, which gave them a strange kind of look, but this was done so that the little teddy could see over the top of the soldier's pocket. Other English makers also produced Soldier Bears, including a company that little is known about named Steevans. We do know that the company flourished from 1910 to the early 1920s and that some of their early bears are labelled, but most of them are not. Their Soldier Bears were made much more crudely than those of Farnell, meaning that very few have survived to this day, and which also means that they are in high demand by collectors.

The saddest thing about these little bears is that many returned home with their companions and many returned home alone, but many died alongside their companions on the battlefields.

Farnell also produced little 'Soldier Dogs' and 'Soldier Cats' alongside the little bears. They looked a lot like the teddy bears and it is interesting to learn that the author A. A. Milne (author of *Winnie-the-Pooh*) carried a little soldier dog to war with him, named Carmen. Apparently, his wife Daphne slipped the little dog into his bag on his last morning in England before leaving to fight abroad.

We can only imagine just how important war teddies were to their companions during those most terrible of times and I am always amazed at some of the stories that surround these old bears. One such teddy, named Cecil, now lives at the Fairlynch Museum in Devon. Born in South Africa in 1907, he joined the Great Bear Regiment in Canada in 1915. Tired after a battle, he crawled into a hole to sleep, the hole being the muzzle of a German field gun. The gun was immediately put out of action, so you could say he did his bit for the war effort. Cecil later went to live in India, where unfortunately cockroaches ate one of his ears. He was later bequeathed to the Fairlynch Museum by Miss C. Elgee. It was her father who carried him in his knapsack throughout the First World War.

When the war ended the teddy bear had certainly not lost his popularity; in fact, demand for him had grown. However, despite their best efforts companies found it hard to recover, mostly because of the shortages of materials. Manufacturers used whatever resources they could to keep the industry going and in Germany at the Steiff

Above left & right: Tommy, a Soldier Bear made by the English company Steevans Manufacturing Co. Ltd in around 1915. Tommy was originally owned by a soldier who was a medic during the war.

Cecil, a teddy bear mascot from the First World War.
(Image courtesy of the Fairlynch Museum, Devon)

Commemorative china makers soon realised the potential
of the teddy bear craze, as with these examples dated
c. 1909.

factory this went to a greater level. Luckily, Paul, Richard, Hugo and Otto (who were all management) returned home, but traditional toy making materials had all but dried up. They looked around for new materials they could use, even trying nettles and wood – something the country was rich in – to make coverings for their bears and toys, but who would ever believe that a teddy bear could be made from wood? Well, experiments were carried out and resulted in a unique teddy bear that was made of 'paper plush', and today these bears are some of the most sought-after teddy bears ever. It is reported that some 19,556 paper plush teddy bears were made between the years 1919 and 1922. For some of us who would love to get our hands on one of these bears, we were lucky that Steiff recreated this famous bear in 2009, although he was limited edition and could only be obtained by a few lucky bear lovers.

Manufacturers really struggled for a while and when they finally got back on their feet we found the teddy bear had started to change his looks, often quite dramatically. Many early bears had shoe/boot button eyes that were made of wood (the very early ones were made of metal), but this had started to change and clear glass eyes with black pupils were now very popular. At the start of the twentieth century, many British soft toy companies began producing teddy bears and many of the larger ones are very well documented, making it relatively easy to identify their bears, and many of these companies also put labels or buttons or both on their bears. However, there was also a large number of smaller toy companies who made teddy bears but who only survived for a very short time, and these firms never bothered keeping records or used labels to identify their bears, and so today we do have lots of teddy bears out there that we find almost impossible to identify. We can only look at body shape, eyes, noses and the like to roughly identify their age, but I would emphasise that this is not always a bad thing for collectors as we love the mystery that these old teddy bears carry.

When materials were in short supply, the German makers Steiff came up with the paper plush teddy bear.

An early one-eared, English-made teddy bear. Fortunately, there are many collectors who rescue these forgotten bears.

An early English bear named Oliver, dating from *c.* 1917.

The 1920s was certainly a very exciting time for the teddy bear. In 1920, the editor of the *Daily Express*, R. D. Blumenfeld, was instructed by the newspaper owner, Lord Beaverbrook, to launch a comic strip that would outshine those of rival papers. Blumenfeld commissioned Mary Tourtel (wife of the night-news editor) who was already a well-known illustrator of children's books. She came up with the idea of Rupert Bear (that very sweet little bear who was dressed in checked trousers and scarf). Rupert first appeared in the *Daily Express* on 8 November 1920 in a story called *The Adventures of a Little Lost Bear.*

Rupert Bear was originally created by Mary Tourtel in 1920. He made his first appearance in the *Daily Express* on 8 November 1920.

Was it bears like Rupert who started the craze of dressing teddies? At the end of the First World War it became popular to cut up uniforms and make clothes for your old teddy bear. From his very early years the teddy has always been an ideal candidate for dressing up like a human. Both adults and children alike seem to love the idea of dressing their bears, sometimes like themselves. For children it meant that their teddy bear took on a more human form in their imagination and for adults dressing their old bears seems to give them a much better stance in life (it also helps to protect older bears from dust and handling, so I would definitely recommend it!)

Some of the world's best-loved teddy bears were made during the 1920s and 1930s; in fact, it was a boom time for the teddy bear, and not only was he beginning to acquire a new look, but his stuffing, which had previously been wood-shavings (which were used as packing material for china and known in the United States as 'excelsior') and even pieces of cork and horsehair, was now changing. Now a lighter filling was being used, a stuffing named kapok that was a fine cotton-like material that is harvested from the seed-pod of the tropical tree *Ceiba pentandra* and was originally used to stuff cushions and even lifejackets.

Some of the best known and now very collectable teddy bears from this era were made by the German company Schuco. Founded in Nuremberg in 1912, this company was famous for producing toy monkeys as well as teddy bears. It was to be their Piccolo range of bears and monkeys that proved the most popular. Measuring just over 3 inches tall, they came onto the market in 1926. Many contained a scent bottle that ladies of those times loved to keep in their handbag, and some were made with a pin on their back, so they could be attached to a lapel and used to squirt water, as

Ted Hart, a Merrythought bear from 1958, who is still owned and loved by his original owner.

Eileen's Bear, a gorgeous old Chiltern teddy who lived above a grocery shop in Gloucester.

An unidentified old bear from *c.* 1920 (with new ears), known as Watford.

Gordon. Old bears take on great character over the years because of the way they are loved and handled.

a joke. When these particular little bears come on to the market today they are often described as scent atomisers, rather than as cute little water pistols. Later these bears were also made to hold a small bottle of spirit, although it is thought that these would have been used for advertising purposes. We do know for certain that the company originally produced them as an advertising promotion for the Shell Oil Company. Another feature of these sweet little teddies was their colour; they were produced in a variety of wonderful colours including pink, red, gold and lilac, as well as usual teddy bear colours. They remained on sale for many years and today they are possibly not as rare as you might think, but these tiny teddies are great for collectors who are short of space and have as much character and charm as teddy bears a hundred times their size.

One British company who had a similar history to that of Farnell was W. J. Terry. At the turn of the century this company made soft toys using real fur, as did many others. By 1909, after its success with a toy dog named Terry'er that was based on King Edward VII's dog Caesar, the company opened a large factory in London and in 1913 added teddy bears to their catalogue. Their teddies, who were now made from mohair, had glass eyes like those of Farnell's, web claws like those of Farnell and a hump on their back, like Farnell, but W. J. Terry bears lacked the quality of those bears made by Farnell, which is probably why there are many more Farnell bears out there who have survived than those of W. J. Terry. Still, it is not always easy to tell these two makers apart. In 1924, upon the death of William Terry, his son Frederick struggled to keep the business going. Like so many other companies it was then hit very hard by the Great Depression, which struck in the early 1930s. Subsequently, W. J. Terry, along with countless other small companies, was forced to close its doors.

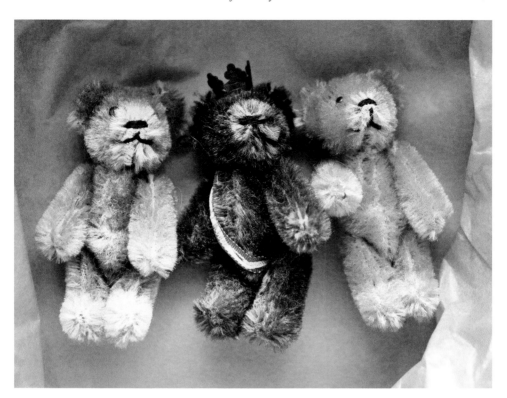

Tiny Schuco bears from the 1920s. These bears are now extremely popular with collectors. Many of these bears concealed all sorts of useful items.

Ed is an early W. J. Terry bear who lost an ear many moons ago.

The Great Depression

It was during the early 1920s that the United States especially was booming financially and businesses of all kinds were starting up everywhere. Immigrants from all parts of the world came flooding into the Land of Opportunity, but this was to change overnight in October of 1929 when millions of dollars were wiped off the stock market in what history now calls the Wall Street Crash. Repercussions of this were felt all over the world, including in England, and is better known in our history books as the Great Depression. Once again, the course of the teddy bear's journey was hit heavily on both sides of the Atlantic. As people were cutting back severely on all expenditure, teddy bears were considered a luxury item that could be done without. The companies that did survive had to start producing teddy bears from cheaper materials to sell at the lower end of the market, if they were to survive at all. Looking at the makers Farnell again, they were also constantly being undercut by European imports. The whole situation lasted until 1933, when once again new businesses started up. Back in the United States, New York's famous Ideal Novelty Company (the first US teddy bear makers) did somehow seem to survive, along with the Knickerbocker Toy Company, which was founded in Albany, New York, in 1850. This company started out producing educational toys but later they too produced teddy bears. Now you may think that 'Knickerbocker' is a strange name for a toy company, but Dutch Settlers in New York were often called Knickerbockers because of the puffed-out trousers they once wore, hence the company's name.

Bobby is an early teddy bear with no
identifiable marks; well-loved, he has very
little fur left on his old body.

Whenever I invite people to bring along their old teddy bears to a lecture, undoubtedly the most popular old bears of all are those made by Chiltern and this is probably because they were made to a very high standard, which means not only did they survive lots of love and cuddles, tears and adventures, but also the test of time.

Chiltern Toys was originally formed in Germany in 1881 as a toy export company. It all started with two brothers, Josef (who lived in London) and Gabriel Eisenmann (who lived in Germany). In 1900 Leon Rees joined Josef as a business partner and later married his daughter. The company, Eisenmann & Co. Ltd, brought teddy bears into England from Germany. In 1908 Eisenmann opened the Chiltern Works, although it was mostly dolls being produced. When the First World War began and German bears were banned from entering Britain, Chiltern turned its attention to making teddy bears. The first teddy bear was named Master Teddy and it was first seen in 1915. This bear was truly very different; it looked like no other teddy bear of its time, with its googly eyes and strange but very happy face, but it was a great success.

Eisenmann also produced some bears under the name of 'Einco', and yet again these bears looked an awful lot like those of Farnell. Leon Rees later took over his father-in-law's business and joined forces with Harry Stone (who was a former director of J. K. Farnell). It worked well, with Rees taking charge of marketing and Stone taking care of design. The first toys to be marketed under the Chiltern Toys label were in 1923 and included the now extremely popular Chiltern Hugmee Bears.

Above: Steve Zodiac is an old Chiltern bear from the 1920s, showing the distinctive raised stitches at each side of his nose.

Left: A Master Teddy replica.

An old Chiltern bear named Claude
Albert from the 1950s.

Chiltern Hugmee Bears

So popular with collectors today, these adorable bears started life in 1923 and were
Chiltern's most famous range of teddy bears. Named after the labels worn by early
bears – 'Hug Me and I'll Growl' – they were made up until the 1960s. Most of them
were made from golden mohair, although they were made in other colours too,
including some pastel shades. Early Hugmee Bears had long and often shaved muzzles,
along with long arms, bodies that were filled with kapok, heads filled with wood wool
and velvet (or cotton) paw pads, while their noses had characteristic upward stitches
at either side. As time passed their design changed slightly; for example, the feet pads
were later made of rexine (an imitation leather used on many bears, not just Chiltern).
Rexine looked good when it was new but after a while it peeled off either partially or
completely, leaving just a woven backing which you see on many old teddy bears today.
During the late 1950s/60s they were given the now famous black plastic noses, which
were reputedly taken from toy dogs that were also being made at the factory at the
same time. These little black noses were a great success, especially as they conformed
to the new safety regulations (something we will look at later on).

I cannot move on from the 1920s without touching upon the story of possibly the
most important teddy bear ever, a teddy who is now known as the Patron Saint of
Teddy Bears; his name of course is Winnie-the-Pooh. Despite the rounded and yellow
body that we have all come to love in the story books, the real Winnie was a gorgeous
mohair teddy bear made by the English soft toy company Farnell.

Toad is a very sweet old Chiltern Hugmee Bear from the 1950s, and features the famous black plastic nose that is loved by collectors.

An old Farnell teddy named Billy Moon from
c. 1920s, visiting 'The Enchanted Forest' where the
young Christopher Robin played with his famous
bear, Winnie-the-Pooh.

The year was 1921 when a van load of teddy bears was delivered to the London store of Harrods, and among them was a teddy who was to lead a life brimming full of adventures, and who would later be loved by people, both young and old, all around the world. When the bears were taken to the toy department on the first floor, it was by chance that a young mother named Daphne Milne was to enter the store looking for a special gift for her son's first birthday, and made the decision to buy him a Farnell teddy. When he arrived at his new home the teddy was given to Daphne's son, Christopher Robin Milne, and was named Edward Bear (later to have a name change to Winnie-the-Pooh). From that day on the two were practically inseparable, and so began their adventures together in Ashdown Forest.

Winnie has amazingly survived to this day despite all his adventures and he can still be seen residing at the New York Public Library, in the Children's Section there. He lives in a large glass cabinet along with his old pals. I have been lucky enough to visit him on a number of occasions, and although I would love to have him living back here in England, I can honestly say he looks very safe, and what better way for a teddy bear like him to spend his later years than being surrounded by children?

A discreet bronzed plaque can be found at Gills Lap as a memorial to the unique friendship of Christopher Robin and Pooh Bear.

New York Public Library, which is now the permanent home to Christopher Robin Milne's bear, Winnie-the-Pooh, and his friends.

Winnie-the-Pooh now resides with his friends in the Children's Room of the New York Public Library.

Earning His Keep

Since his very early years, teddy has earned his keep in the field of advertising, but during the 1920s onwards even more so. The company Bear Brand Stockings, which had its main offices in Chicago, had for some unknown reason used a grizzly bear in their advertising campaign. When nylon stockings became all the rage the company decided it was time to look for a new icon and chose to use a Chad Valley teddy bear, who they named Chad. Dressed in his black top hat and carrying a walking cane, he really was every bit the gentleman and was very true of his time. Advertisements for nylons with his cute face became well known all over the world.

Bear brand stockings were frequently advertised in shop windows. The Chad Valley bear shown here, *c.* 1960s, is named Brian.

Chad Valley

Teddy bears made by this company just happen to be among my favourite. Chad Valley was another company which was more or less pushed into teddy bear production because of the lack of teddy bears in England during the First World War. The company had originally started out as Johnson Bros, a bookbinding and printing business working from Handsworth. In 1860 Joseph and Alfred Johnson set up a similar business in Birmingham and in 1897, Joseph, along with his son, moved to Harborne to set up their own business, only this time producing board games and later on stationery and soft toys. In 1915 the company added a teddy bear to its catalogue. During the First World War the British Government was very enthusiastic to boost morale, ensuring that products like the teddy bear that had previously been imported from Germany were now being produced in Britain and supported businesses like this as much as they could. The company was by now calling itself Chad Valley and was producing some very individual and very beautiful teddy bears. By 1920 the company had opened a factory called the Wrekin Toy Works in Wellington, Shropshire, and its main emphasis was on its teddy bears. It was actually Chad Valley who later went on to earn the right to put a label on its bears stating 'Royal Warrant of Appointment as Toymakers to Her Majesty the Queen' in 1938, which was certainly a very big honour that I have to say was more than well deserved. I love these bears.

A 'button-in-ear' early Chad Valley Bear named Peter from *c.* 1920.

Moving On

We have talked about German bears, English bears and bears from the United States, but by now many other countries had started to bring their versions of the teddy bear to the market, including France. The very first French teddy bear maker was Pintel et Fils. Marcel Pintel began making soft toys as far back as 1913 for his father's Paris-based business. Marcel was a very competitive young man who was determined to produce soft toys that were better than all the others he saw on the market. In 1911 his first mechanical tumbling clown came on to the market but the First World War hit production. However, Marcel later developed a range of mohair bears, which appeared on the market in 1920. Pintel teddy bears were delicate, with tapering French flair. People loved these bears and demand for them was so great that production had to be outsourced.

Talking of clowns, teddy bear clowns were incredibly popular during the 1920s. Richard Steiff inspired the first brightly coloured bears, who were made in pink, yellow and tipped mohair, and were patented by Steiff in 1926. They were kapok-filled and contained a press-type voice box. Original Teddy Clowns wore fabric frills around their necks and wonderful conical hats that were decorated with pom-poms. Steiff was said to have produced some 30,000 Teddy Clowns between 1926 and 1928.

A hug of Steiff Teddy Clowns.

Two really loved old French teddy bears named Quinn (the larger bear) and Marcel.

The Thirties

The year was 1930, and despite the financial issues in the world, one very famous English soft toy company was about to start its life. The company I am referring to, Merrythought, still nestles its factory in a small town called Ironbridge in Shropshire. It has become one of the world's best loved and best-known makers of teddy bears, and it is a company that has always been popular with the Royal Family too.

   The story of Merrythought all began a long time ago with two men, W. G. Holmes and H. G. Laxton, partners in a worsted spinning mill based at Vale Mills, Oakworth, in Yorkshire that began in 1919. The factory produced the finest mohair from raw materials that were imported from both South Africa and Turkey. They decided to open their own soft toy factory, producing toys made from their own mohair, but first they needed to find both suitable premises and someone with experience in the soft toy business to run this new venture. They found C. J. Rendle, who had previously worked at Chad Valley Toys as Head of Production. With him he brought a number of other skilled workers, among them a lady named Florence Attwood, who was to become responsible for design. Attwood created many designs that were innovative and ensured

A Merrythought corgi dog from *c.* 1950s. His name is Charlie.

that Merrythought survived throughout difficult years. What was even more impressive about this lady was the fact that she was deaf, and in those days the attitude of people to others with disabilities was far less enlightened than today. Having lost her hearing at the age of two after a bout of measles, the little girl also discovered that her speech had been affected too. Throughout her early years Florence chose to use sign language, but she was not mute, as many believe. Born in Shropshire in 1907, she was offered a place at the Royal School for the Deaf in Manchester in 1915. About two years later she met another deaf girl from Shropshire who was quite a bit younger than Florence and they became very good friends (probably due to travelling back and forth from Manchester to Shropshire together). The young girl was called Catherine Mavis Rendle and was the daughter of Clifton Rendle, who at that time was working in a senior position at Chad Valley Works in Wellington. When Florence finished her training in 1926 Rendle repaid her kindness to his daughter by employing her as a toy maker at Chad Valley. Of course, when he left to join the new company Merrythought, she went too. It was around 1948 when Florence became ill and she sadly died in 1952 at the age of just forty-four.

The very first teddy bear to come out of the Merrythought factory was in 1930. The business was originally started in hired rooms at the Station Hotel in Wellington, until premises that were suitable could be found. In February 1931 the company moved into permanent premises at the site of the Old Coalbrookdale Iron Foundry on the banks of the River Severn. The 1930s was a very busy time for Merrythought, like other makers in England such as Chad Valley and Chiltern, and Merrythought was to become the largest soft toy company in England. In 1933 it expanded again, with orders for toys and teddy bears pouring in.

An early Merrythought teddy bear named Cider at his manufacturer's birthplace, Ironbridge in Shropshire.

Merrythought 'Chummy' bear from
c. 1930s, with the celluloid button-in-ear.

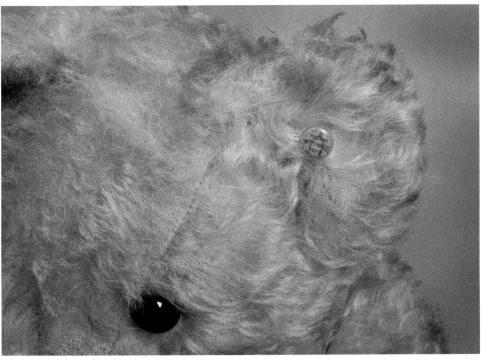

The Second World War

The teddy bear had by now certainly made his mark on the toy world, taking over every heart in his path. Children everywhere adored him, and adults too, but then along came the Second World War. Just like the First World War, teddy bear production was hit hard. Merrythought was taken over by the Admiralty for mapmaking and so for a while the company moved back to Wellington, where it produced fabric for war items, such as gas masks and sleeve badges. Meanwhile, back in Germany factories were still trying to recover from the First World War and the economic crisis that followed had certainly not helped. At Steiff many employees were called up for war duties, leaving the company yet again with a shortage of both materials (especially plush) and workers. Richard Steiff had by then emigrated to the United States to help the overseas division,

Bert; some old bears are difficult to date unless some of their history is known.

and the company wondered how it would manage. In May 1943 production at Steiff ceased completely to make way for munitions work (toy making did not resume until October 1945). The small town of Giengen, which was by now in the hands of American troops, and the factory were raided often for souvenirs to take back home to America. Fortunately, an unknown person had packed away the Steiff archives in wooden boxes and hidden them in unused garages. It is because of this that nearly every teddy bear ever produced by the company is now in the company's archives, along with patterns.

Children at War

Throughout the long days and nights of the Second World War, children relied upon their teddy bears to give them comfort and support, and this he did with courage and valour, determined to serve his young companions. If ever a toy deserved a medal, the teddy bear did. Children who were evacuated from their family and friends needed a teddy bear so very much as he was to be their one link with home. He stayed beside his child companion always, never flinching, never letting go. He was indeed their trooper. Many teddy bears who were companions of children during those terrible times became lost or mislaid and have never been seen since by their owners. Many teddy bears during those times were even shared by children, but whatever the circumstances one thing is for absolute certain: he was and will always be remembered by them. It wasn't just children who needed the love and support of a teddy during those terrible times, however; by now he became a friend and confidante to anyone who needed him, including airmen, soldiers and many other people who were risking their lives doing valuable war work.

The East London Federation Toy Factory was founded in 1914 in Bow by the suffragette Sylvia Pankhurst (daughter of the famous Emmeline 'Emily' Pankhurst). The company's early products consisted of rag dolls among other goods, most of which were designed by artists who were commissioned from the Chelsea Polytechnic. It was important to Pankhurst to employ women and to pay them fair wages for the work they did. In 1921 the word 'Federation' was dropped from the name of the company and in 1926 it registered the name Ealontoys as its trading name (later to become the company name in 1948). Teddy bears appeared in their catalogue in 1924; these bears were made of good quality materials and were very successful and by 1950 Ealontoys actually called themselves the Teddy Bear People in all of their advertising slogans. Their teddies have very heavy square noses and V-shaped mouths, which many collectors believe give them a sad look. However, along with many other small toy companies, they hit heavy financial troubles after the war years and so were forced to close their doors in the early 1950s. One interesting point is that although this company produced both dolls and teddy bears, and many other toys too, they never produced toys they believed to be weapons of war, such as toy guns.

As well as being renowned for never leaving his companion's side, the teddy bear is also renowned for keeping secrets, and during the war years this, of course, was very important, especially if you worked for a top-secret base that was set up in the heart of the Buckinghamshire countryside that was to prove a particularly important part of the war years. The special base I am relating to was known as Station X, which is probably better known to us all now as Bletchley Park, home to the famous Enigma decoding machine. It was certainly hard for the people who worked there as, not only could they

Made of silk plush, this old bear, named Kristopher, was made sometime during the 1930s.

Harold, who was probably made by Farnell to the same pattern as their Soldier Bears, although this old guy is larger, standing at 5 inches tall.

An old, dressed English teddy
named Peggy.

never discuss their work at home with family or friends, but they could never discuss their work with each other. This resulted in many who worked at the base having a teddy bear companion to share their secrets with. We know that Alan Turing had a teddy bear who he called Porgy and, after careful research, we know there were many others. I came across a wonderful little teddy bear named Winston who belonged to a lady who worked on many top-secret bases during the war years, including Bletchley. Previously, she had lost all her belongings and home during the Blitz, so her little teddy bear must have been incredibly valuable to her. While working at Bletchley, she carried the little teddy bear with her in her handbag so that she always had someone to talk to and share those precious secrets with. What she told little Winston, of course, we shall never know.

The Second World War was truly a very difficult time for the teddy bear. True, a few back-room makers set up in business making very small ranges of teddy bears from some very cheap materials that were available to them. Wounded servicemen who were recovering in hospitals were also encouraged to make soft toys and teddy bears, although the only type of material available to them was a fabric known as American Cloth, which was not a pleasant material to handle, but these bears were quite desirable

He measures just a few inches tall, but
Winston, a roughly made little English
bear, was the companion of a lady who
worked at Bletchley Park during the
Second World War.

because of the bright colours used. Unfortunately, not many of these bears survived because the material cracked very quickly. Probably the most popular teddy bear that appeared during the Second World War was the one made by a mother, grandmother or auntie. This teddy bear was either knitted from recycled yarn or made from recycled materials. Many magazines of the time published patterns for handmade teddy bears. Although not worth very much, these teddy bears are some of the most special, precious and personal teddy bears that ever were, because so much love was put into every stitch. A few of these teddies survive to this day but sadly I don't yet have one in my collection.

When this war finally came to an end, manufacturers very quickly began to pick up the pieces and start production again because demand had not stopped or even subsided. In 1946 soft toy and teddy bear production once again started at the Merrythought factory, only this time under the management of B. Trayton Holmes (son of one of the original founders). Times were still very hard due to the shortages of materials, but things for Merrythought got even harder as during that same year the River Severn burst its banks and flooded the factory, taking most of the stock with it. However, despite the bad luck suffered by this company, it somehow managed to recover by the following year, producing a catalogue that featured some of its pre-war designs. These teddy bears were known as M. Bears.

Many soft toy companies used any surplus materials they could lay their hands on at the end of the war to make their teddy bears, including army blankets, uniforms and even surplus buttons. One wonderful story is told by a son whose mother worked for Farnell before the war. He remembers his mother starting production of teddy bears once again after the war, only this time she worked from her front room. He remembers people knocking on her front door and handing over old flying jackets, which she would cut up to use the sheepskin for stuffing and the leather for making the bears' paw pads.

At the end of the war Austria started producing teddy bears, with a few of these companies again using up surplus materials. However, when the problems of the war years began to ease sometime during the 1950s, mohair was once again used. The makers Berg began making bears in 1946 and William Fechter started making bears

An old pattern from the Second World War.
Making a teddy bear from scraps of material often
recycled material.

A Merrythought bear from the 1930s (with
button in ear), a bear which is sought after by
today's collectors.

An early Farnell bear
named Joey.

around the same time as Berg. In 1978 the Fechter factory closed its doors but the
Berg factory carried on to become Austria's largest producers of teddy bears. The early
Berg bears had voice boxes that were truly the work of ingenuity and comprised a very
simply made pouch that contained loose pebbles.

The company Invicta was founded in 1935 by G. E. Beer and T. B. Wright, with the
name coming from the Latin word *invicti,* which means unconquerable and unbeaten.
Beer had previously been a director and designer and Wright a sales representative
for Farnell. It's funny how the name Farnell keeps turning up and how the name links
itself to so many other manufacturers. Invicta was quite a large company, employing
around 300 members of staff. In 1936 Beer bought Wright out and just before the
war the company produced lovely mohair teddy bears with glass eyes (a lot like those
of Farnell, really). During the war years the factory, which was based in Park Royal
Road, North West London, was used by the military to make armaments, but a few
employees were taken to a disused laundry close by to carry on producing a limited
number of soft toys. When the war ended, the company made their bears from wool
plush, using rexine for their paw pads. The business closed its doors in 1954.

A jointed bear made from cotton plush fabric and probably of Polish origin.

Davey is a cute German bear.

Perry, who was made by Invicta, still has much of his original fur coat left.

The Fifties and Sixties

The year was 1953; among all the street parties, the jelly, the cheers and the shouts, and among the gold and glitter of the Coronation of Queen Elizabeth II, stood a little teddy bear who was made in the patriotic colours of red, white and blue. The teddy was made by a couple of English makers, one of which was Merrythought, and he took his place among the ever so many novelties and souvenirs made for the day. However, it was not the first time this little teddy bear had been made. Back in 1937, trade papers say that Farnell made similar bears for the crowning of George VI (following the abdication of his brother, Edward VII).

The Merrythought Coronation Bear, made in the patriotic colours of red, white and blue.

The teddy bear became a trend-setter during the 1960s. He could often be seen having his photograph taken alongside many celebrities, including pop-stars, actors and top models of the day. He was also being seen more and more as a mascot for sportsmen and women, including the late Donald Campbell, who was a compulsive record breaker on land and sea during the 1950s and 1960s using cars named *Bluebird*. Whenever Donald went for a record attempt, so too did his little bear, Mr Whoppit, a foxy-looking little bear made by Merrythought. Together they broke the water speed record seven times and survived many near fatal crashes, but sadly on 4 January 1967, when he was going for a speed record at Coniston Water, tragedy struck and both Campbell and Whoppit sank deep into the water. Somehow Whoppit survived the crash (we think because his stuffing was buoyant) and he floated to the surface a short time later. He then went on to undertake more record attempts with Campbell's daughter, Gina.

The 1960s was a decade when the teddy bear started to change his shape again, only this time quite dramatically. For a start the materials he was now being made from, as a result of developments in the field of plastics, totally revolutionised the way he was made. By 1960 many well-loved makers were using woven and later knitted nylon plush to make their bears. The Deans Rag Book Company, for example, made a De-Luxe Bri-Nylon teddy bear in 1965 (the word Bri-Nylon being a bit of an 'in-word' of the times). Bri-Nylon was the registered trademark of ICI, the makers of various synthetic fabrics. The American-owned company Monsato produced a fabric named Acrilan (woven from acrylic fabrics). You see, new fabrics had to be found for making teddy bears because he now faced yet another big threat on his journey through time, and the threat this time was something called Health and Safety Regulations.

For the first time since his creation, the teddy bear was starting to be unloved by a certain few. His eyes, which were often made of glass and fitted to the bear using metal stalks, were not considered safe for children anymore, and his fillings were dangerous and considered dirty for children to cuddle up to. Health and Safety issues were slowly removing the child's relationship with teddy and because of this his popularity started to decline. Then along came a company who revolutionised the teddy bear – Wendy Boston.

It all began in January 1909 in Acocks Green, Birmingham. Nora Wendy Boston grew up in a family that was used to business and commerce. Her father Ernest was a coal merchant and her mother, Nora Jenkins, was a part of the Jenkins Silver Company, which owned a factory in Birmingham. The young Wendy studied at the Lawnside Art College and later went on to work at the famous Cadbury's factory, where her job was to produce promotional materials. Later, she married Ken Williams and everything was fine with the newly married couple until the war started and Ken joined the RAF. During 1941 he was invalided out and then worked for a number of retail stores and pubs until their house was bombed. It was then that both Ken and Wendy decided it was the right time to move on, so they did, moving to a small town just outside of Abergavenny in Wales called Crickhowell. Due to the shortages that the war years brought, Wendy made some toys for friend's children out of any old scarps of material that she could find, including old blankets. Friends thought these toys were rather special and Ken, who was never one to miss a business opportunity, took a box of Wendy's toys to a Cardiff department store, who it seems bought the lot from him straight away for a whopping £100 – an awful lot of money in those times. In 1945,

Mr Whoppit is shown here with his record-breaking companion Gina Campbell (daughter of the famous Donald Campbell).

A soft plush teddy made by Deans between 1957 and 1961, showing how his shape had changed.

a company was formed with one lock-up shop, one female employee and of course Ken, who handled the running of the business. They used Wendy's maiden name for the business, Wendy Boston (Crickhowell) Limited.

The popular fabric of those times was nylon, which had been invented in 1935, but up until this time no one had thought about using it to produce soft toys. Ken approached Norton Weaving (Yorkshire) Limited to ask them if they could supply a nylon plush for his toys. The stuffing of toys was also a big issue of the time, and on a visit to Woolworths Ken noticed some washable foam and brought a bag back to the factory, where he experimented with slicing it into strips and later into cubes. The foam was dustless, springy and very quick to dry when wet. It was 1954 when the Wendy Boston Teddy was first launched and in 1955 he was even making appearances on the BBC. As well as producing a new fully washable teddy bear that could even be put through a mangle (please don't try this today!), the company also introduced modern safety eyes, which were made of plastic and could be screw-locked into the teddy's head. These eyes also had rust-proofed nuts.

The company's premises were soon to become much too small to accommodate the business and so another factory was opened nearby in Abergavenny, although not long after these premises were opened they were devastated by fire. Not only was the site destroyed, but with it three large export orders and tons of raw materials, amounting in total to some £20,000 in damages and loss. However, stock books and order books were rescued, having been stored in metal cabinets, and the company somehow managed to recover.

The revolutionary Wendy Boston bears were certainly a new generation of teddy.

The site of the first Wendy Boston factory (now a hardware shop) in Crickhowell.

Stella with promotional lamb made for Lister Woo

A member of the Wendy
Boston staff.

Wendy Boston bears sold in their thousands over the next few years. During the
height of the company's trading, some 27 per cent of all toys exported from the UK
and up to half of those toys sold domestically were made by this company. The
workers were mostly all female and at one time numbered 250, many of them joining
the business upon leaving school, so many of the girls were very young and from the
so-called 'Swinging Sixties'. Ken came up with the idea of playing modern music in
the factory while the girls worked, which he maintained kept them happy. Ken also
arranged coach trips for the workforce to see celebrities of that time, such as Harry
Secombe and Brian Rix. The company certainly prospered and teamed up with the
company Hoover, who gave a 'Certificate of Washability' for their toys as it was a

Hoover mangle that Ken operated when he attended toy fairs. By 1959 competitors began making their version of child-safe toys and teddy bears and cheap foreign imports had also started to hit the teddy bear market. Soon the safety and hygiene theme used by Wendy Boston started to slip away. Wendy's habit of chain-smoking had started to take its toll on her health and Ken was finding it increasingly difficult to both run the now ailing business and take care of his sick wife, which very sadly resulted in the company running up large debts. An approach was made in 1968 by Denys Fisher to buy the business and this resulted in the sale of the Wendy Boston company for little more than the amount of the debts. Sadly, in 1972 Wendy Boston died.

The late 1950s and early 1960s was an exciting time for the teddy bear despite the sad fact that many famous names were forced to close their doors due to cheap foreign imports that were playing havoc with the industry. New ideas had to be found and during this time many exciting, colourful and new designs were to hit the market.

These bears were not only fully washable, but could also be put through a mangle.

McLeod is a vintage teddy made in America by the famous Ideal Company.

Punks

Have you ever wondered how punks got their name? Well, one of Canada's most famous animators, Charlie Thorson – who, by the way, was the designer of Bugs Bunny and Disney's Snow White – was commissioned to create a character by the department store Eatons who would challenge Rudolph. He came up with a character named Punkinhead, or Punkie. This character was a cub-like bear who made his debut in Christmas 1949. Punkie led the Toronto Christmas Parade, which at that time was the biggest in North America, and over a million people came to see him. His success also meant that he could now be used in television commercials, for children's books and toys for the famous store. The English toymaker Merrythought, who already supplied Eatons with many of their toys, was approached to make the character into a teddy bear, with the job being given to Florence Attwood. Punkinhead's production ceased in 1956, when Eatons looked for a new character, although thankfully Merrythought have produced more of these characters in recent years.

Punkinhead.

Cheeky Bears

It is said that Punkinhead gave way to one of the world's most iconic teddy bears. It was June Barker who was to take over from Attwood and in 1957, just one year after the cessation of Punkinhead, she introduced a bear named Tubby Bear. Although this bear was designed by June, she did give the bear the archive prefix FA/JB, probably, we believe, as an acknowledgement of Attwood's bear Punkinhead, who obviously played a big part in Tubby Bear's design. When Tubby Bear was exhibited at a toy fair, he was singled out by a member of the Royal Family who came to visit; reportedly, Queen Elizabeth II. It is also reported that she picked up the little teddy bear and said, 'What a cheeky little bear,' and the name stuck.

Since that important date in teddy bear history for this Merrythought bear, he seems to have rocked the world. Collectors around the world simply cannot get enough of him, with his big infectious smile, velvet muzzle and the bells in his ears. Cheeky Bear

Right: The Merrythought Cheeky Bear, *c*. 1960 – a new style of teddy bear. These bears are still being made and are as popular as they ever were with collectors.

Below: Virgin Atlantic used a Cheeky Bear for the year 2000.

has many famous fans around the world both past and present, including the late Dusty Springfield who, when asked by music presenter Emperor Rosko in 1970, 'Who is your best friend?', responded that it was Mr Einstein, her old Cheeky Bear. Talking of the Royal Family and teddy bears, the company Merrythought has always had a bit of a connection. For example, did you know that Prince Edward gave Prince Andrew and his bride Sarah Ferguson each a very large Merrythought teddy bear on the day of their wedding? The bears then rode with them in their wedding carriage.

Louis is a typical classic teddy bear from the 1960s. Although made by Merrythought, note that some of his features look like a bear made by Chad Valley.

Along Came the Seventies

Along came the seventies, bringing with it more problems for the poor teddy bear. To start with the birth rate had fallen, and to add to this children no longer wanted the old-fashioned toys of the past, wanting instead more modern toys like space hoppers and board games like Simon. We were now looking at the beginning of high-tech toys. When the 1970s arrived, most of the wonderful toy makers from days gone by had been crushed by cheap imports arriving on the scene – companies like Pedigree Soft Toys, who had evolved from the famous Triang Toys, one of the most recognised names in the toy industry and in the history of British toy making, Triang being an off shoot of Lines Brothers Limited, a company well known for their quality toys. Established in London during the 1930s, Pedigree expanded rapidly at the end of the war years and many new factories were opened in various parts of the British Empire. The Belfast factory that was opened in 1946 had taken over most of the company's soft toy production by the mid-1950s, but by the mid-1960s the company had become yet another victim of cheap imports.

Alice was made by Pedigree Soft Toys Limited in the 1950s. By this time bears were more often thought of as female.

However, things were by no means all bad during that decade. On the other side of the Atlantic, a teddy bear had started his crusade to win the hearts of the collector's market. Sunny Bear, a brightly coloured teddy bear who was not made of luxury materials and had no special tags or buttons in his ear or anywhere else on his body, was about to become a phenomenon. The whole affair started at the Crocker National Bank in California in 1975. To attract more trade the promotion department came up with the idea of creating some giveaway teddy bears and Sunny Bear was the outcome. The idea was that anyone who opened a checking account of $300 or more could take home a Sunny Bear. The accounts girl Angela Bohring at the Palos Verdes branch said:

It started out great but very soon the problems began. There were teddy bears sitting on the counter as cute as could be and everyone wanted one. Customers who already had accounts insisted they got one. One man who had a fifty-thousand-dollar balance on his account threatened to take out his whole deposit unless he got a bear. We tried to tell him and others just to withdraw three hundred dollars and open another account and some of them did, but mothers would come in with two or three children and each child wanted a bear of course, but it was one account, one bear, so they had

His name is Sunny Bear. He was made as a promotional bear for a Californian bank.

to open two or three checking accounts. On top of everything else a bear shortage began to develop. The top brass sent out a memo that there must be strict accounting for each bear. It soon got so bad that we had a bear account at the end of business each day. The teller had to balance their bears before their drawers. Finally, we had to appoint one of the assistant managers as Bear Man. He would then count them and then lock them up in the bank's vaults overnight. As the bear shortage grew, various branches tried to wheedle more Sunny Bears from others who still had reserves and the Palos Verdes branch had to send out a pick-up truck to a branch in Orange County to bring back more bears (it is rumoured that it carried armed security!). The bank then simply ran out of Sunny Bears in early 1976 but still it was months before the outcry subsided.

In all, some 100,000 Sunny Bears went to bank customers.

Gabrielle Designs

Shirley Clarkson began a business in a spare room of her house in Doncaster, Yorkshire, way back during the recession of the 1970s. What she didn't realise was that her business was destined for international acclaim. It all began quite by accident you see. Shirley was a dab hand at sewing and needlecraft and she would make a soft toy each Christmas for her children, Jeremy (of *Top Gear* fame) and Joanna. It was Christmas 1971 when Jeremy and Joanna received a Paddington Bear. Shirley had based these bears on the books by Michael Bond that her children loved so much. Jeremy and Joanna's friends were so impressed by these bears that Shirley thought there could possibly be a market for them. Shirley and her husband Eddie had just £25 between them to start up a business but, using a cheap sewing machine, she began to produce Paddington Bears and the business simply grew and grew. Later on she employed a couple of local ladies to help her with both the stuffing of these bears as well as the sewing up (she named these ladies 'Stuffers' and 'Plonkers' – a Plonker being a tool used to push stuffing hard into the corners of the bears).

The business soon received orders from major shops around the country, including Hamleys, but at the same time things also started to go a bit wrong as Shirley got involved in some copyright issues. However, after a meeting with Paddington Bear creator Michael Bond, an agreement was reached between them both and business continued. The company was later given the name Gabrielle Designs and the business boomed. Eddie Clarkson gave up his job to work for Shirley full-time and turnover leapt to £1 million a year. Shirley was invited to meet the Queen at the Mansion House in Doncaster because by now her bears had become global celebrities and, of course, she presented one to Her Majesty. She was invited to meet the Queen for a second time in 1994 to celebrate the 800th anniversary of Doncaster being granted a Royal Charter by King John, but this time Shirley had to apologise to the Queen for not bringing her another bear because they had all sold out.

Shirley Clarkson was also the person responsible for giving Paddington Bear a pair of wellington boots. These original boots were made by Dunlop, with paw marks and the letter PB written in reverse on the soles. Michael Bond later wrote these boots into his stories.

Paddington Bear *c.* 1972, made by
Gabrielle Designs.

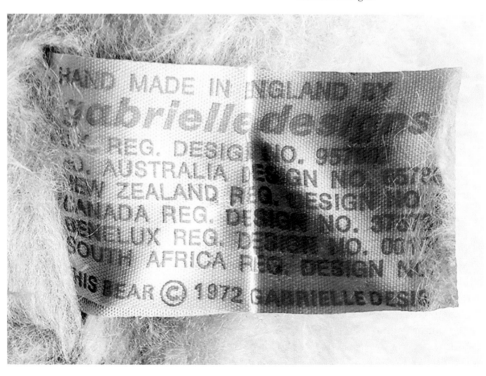

Torville and Dean used a Paddington Bear as their mascot, Twiggy was photographed holding one, Princess Anne was seen holding one after giving birth to her daughter Zara, and when the Channel Tunnel was completed in 1991, a Paddington Bear was passed through to the French side after the initial handshake. Shirley sold the business when Eddie Clarkson died in 1994, and it later went into liquidation – a very sad ending! To this day many of these Paddington Bears still survive and often in very good condition too. Like some of the old teddy bears made by Chiltern, this is probably due to the quality of the materials used to make them. I often see these beautiful bears at collector's fairs, although sadly some of them have lost some or all of their clothes. I am often asked what teddy bears a new collector should be looking to buy and Shirley Clarkson's Paddington Bears are certainly on my list as they have to be up there with the best. Not only are these bears well made, have a great history and are charming character bears, but they are also, at the time of writing this book, very well priced too.

House of Nisbet

The House of Nisbet began life in 1953 as Peggy Nisbet Limited, a company that was famous for producing collector's dolls. The business was situated in Weston-super-Mare. In 1975 the business was taken over by a Canadian called Jack Wilson who was responsible for the name change to House of Nisbet and also for the introduction of teddy bears (originally designed by Peggy Nisbet's daughter, Alison, who later married Jack). A year later the business moved to Dunster Park, near Bristol, and in 1979 began a successful partnership with the late actor/arctophile Peter Bull, who wanted to produce the Teddy Bear of the Century.

It was Peter Bull who originally owned the famous bear named Aloysius from the television series *Brideshead Revisited*. The bear, born in 1907, originally lived with his owner Miss Euphemia Ladd in Sacco, Maine. He had spent some fifty-five years of his life sitting on a shelf in a dry goods and grocery store. His owner, after seeing an interview on television in 1969 where Peter Bull talked about his passion for teddy bears on the *Johnny Carson Show*, decided it was time her bear had a change of life and so she contacted Peter Bull and asked if he would adopt her bear and give him a home. On his arrival Bull named the bear Delicatessen, and when Granada Television held auditions for the series *Brideshead Revisited*, Delicatessen auditioned along with four other bears for the part of Aloysius, the teddy bear who belonged to Evelyn Waugh's character Lord Sebastian Flyte. He got the part almost immediately. On 21 February 1982 Delicatessen's name was changed by deed-poll to Aloysius. In Hollywood he received what just has to be the ultimate accolade when his paw pads were impressed in cement outside Mann's Chinese Theater on Sunset Boulevard.

Sebastian Flyte's bear Aloysius (who is probably named after the Catholic Saint Aloysius Gonzaga) is often mentioned in connection with John Betjeman's childhood teddy bear, which was named Archibald Ormsby-Gore. What many people don't know is that Archibald was actually the inspiration for Evelyn Waugh's character Aloysius, Waugh and Betjeman having met while at Oxford University. Archibald and Betjeman's toy elephant Jumbo were in his arms when he died in 1984.

Bull reproduced his Delicatessen Bear in 1987 using distressed mohair that Jack Wilson helped to invent. Dakin UK bought House of Nisbet out in 1989.

Sailor dolls made by Peggy Nisbet.

Aloysius bears. The larger bear was made by Merrythought and the smaller by House of Nisbet.

The Eighties

When the eighties came along, the teddy bear finally received the credit he was due. This was definitely his decade.

By the 1980s many of our wonderful makers had been lost, but the good news was that many new ones had started. Such was his popularity that by 1984 teddy bear fever had arrived and all major manufacturers created their own special teddies, many of them re-issuing old designs. A survey in Britain revealed that 40 per cent of all teddy bears now sold went to adults and it was during this decade that teddy bears moved from nurseries into the homes and hearts of adults.

Bears were also enjoying their time in the spotlight. One such bear was used as the mascot for the Moscow Olympic Games. The bear, whose name was Misha, won everyone's hearts. You would see him everywhere – on sports clothes, china, postcards and all kinds of souvenirs. However, this bear's road to stardom was not easy. In 1977 the Soviet Olympic Committee asked various artists to draw bears for a competition and out of over a hundred sketches, they chose the one submitted by Victor Chizhikov, liking his bear's smiling face. The bear's creator named him Mikhailo Potapych Toptygin – all three names used for bears from Russian fairy tales. The artist said he thought long and hard as to where the three Olympic rings should be placed and the solution, he said, came to him during a dream when he saw the rings around the bear's waist. The sketch had to be approved first by the Kremlin and afterwards by the then President of the International Olympic Committee, Lord Killanin. The bear was eagerly approved as the official talisman of the 1980 Olympic Games, a bear being a symbol of strength and prowess, two vital ingredients for all athletes. The soft toy Misha was made by the company Dakin, the American company which was taken over by Applause in 1995. If you come across one of these bears, and there are quite a few still around, it is worth adding him to your collection as these bears are quite reasonably priced at present and have a great story to tell.

Manufacturers were quick to react to the ever-increasing teddy bear frenzy that seemed to be rocking the world. With the growth in arctophily, manufacturers turned to the making of limited edition teddy bears. His name was PaPa Bear, he was made in 1980, the first of Steiff's limited edition bears. Only 11,000 of these special bears were produced and only 5,000 of these were made for English-speaking countries. He was based upon Steiff's earliest designs and was made of golden mohair.

These limited edition bears soon began showing up from just about every soft toy manufacturer, many of them being replica bears made from archive patterns and they took the collector's market by storm. British manufacturers like Deans and Merrythought found it increasingly difficult to keep up with demand. Often these limited edition teddy bears were sold out before they even had time to reach the shops;

Misha, the mascot bear of the Moscow
Olympic Games in 1980. He was made by
R. Dakin & Co.

The famous Steiff 'PaPa' bear; the start of a
new generation of limited edition bears to be
made by the company.

bears like Steiff's famous Teddy Rose (1987–88), who was a replica bear of a design originating from 1925 to 1930. These limited edition bears were given a different coloured ear tag to their other bears (which are attached to the company's famous ear button). For example, limited edition bears wore a white ear tag as opposed to the usual yellow tag.

Steiff 'Teddy Rose' with the limited edition black on white label.

The 1980s also saw the collapse of the Berlin Wall in November 1989, and along with it the reunification of Berlin. Like just about every other historical event during his lifetime, the teddy bear was touched, although not in a bad way for once. This time many of the original patterns that had been thought lost were unearthed in forgotten archives.

Some old bears take on a life of adventure. This old English bear is known as Berlin.

The German manufacturers Hermann produced this Berlin Bear, who has a slant on social history.

Artist Bears

Something big also happened during the 1980s. It was the start of a very new market for the teddy bear. As well as the large companies producing their collectable limited edition bears, the new producers were known as teddy bear artists.

So where exactly did teddy bear artistry begin? The true origins are somewhat obscure actually, although we do know that it started in America during the 1970s. Many early teddy bear makers were largely influenced by two English people, one of whom was Margaret Hutchings, who was a journalist working for one of the UK's leading newspapers. In 1964 she produced a book on making teddy bears called *The Book of the Teddy Bear*. The other person responsible, of course, was the actor Peter Bull, who helped make teddy bears acceptable for adults. After appearing on a television chat show (with his teddy bear), the teddy was never again looked at as a child's stuffed toy.

The first teddy bear artist, named Beverley Port, came from the United States. She was the lady who taught many of the famous teddy bear artists of today. Around 1982–83 many aspiring people on both sides of the Atlantic, and indeed in Europe and as far away as Australia, New Zealand and Japan, became attracted to teddy bear making. Their teddy bear creations were as colourful as their imaginations could make them; they were unafraid of using new ideas and mediums, and they were not afraid to be adventurous and disregard conventions. Teddy bear artists, without a doubt, tipped the teddy bear world upside down.

A very colourful artist bear, who shows by her bright pink colour just how far the teddy bear has come since his early years.

Hailing from the 1980s, Just Joey is a very sweet little artist bear.

When the Nineties Arrived

The teddy had certainly made his mark on the world. Manufacturers had started to produce some very different looking bears, maybe because they were inspired by the artist bears that were now taking hold of the market? Merrythought, who we always associated with wonderful classic bears, was now bringing out some very different teddies. One of my favourites was a bear who they named Wellington. He was a very unique looking bear, was made in mohair and came in two sizes. Moreover, he was limited edition, with only 2,500 being made worldwide.

Many larger manufacturers teamed up with some of the most popular teddy bear artists of the day to produce mass-market, limited edition collectable bears. One such bear was named Gregory, who was designed by Carol-Lynn Rossel Waugh and named after her brother for the New York company Effanbee in 1989. However, Effanbee was bought out by Russ Berrie, who introduced her bear Gregory onto the market in 1991. The original Gregory stood some 14 inches tall and was jointed. Russ later brought out a smaller bear who measured just 9 inches tall and was unjointed, although was equally gorgeous.

Wellington. He was made by Merrythought and was launched in their 1991 Collectors Catalogue. He was limited to just 2,500 bears worldwide.

The well-loved Russ 'Gregory' bears. One of Russ's most popular bears from the 1990s, they were made of curly, long-pile synthetic plush.

The sad thing about these bears is I see many of them staring back at me from charity shop baskets with a price tag of just a few pounds. These bears are lovely and belong in the history of teddy bears cabinet. They really are worth taking home with you if you are considering starting a collection. Personally, I love Russ bears and I have a number in my own collection. One of them is a very special bear to me who I named Golden Bear, although his manufacturers actually named him Glimmers.

The origin of Russ bears began in 1963 when Russell Berrie started a business selling novelty items in Palisades Park, a suburb of New York City. He used a converted garage as a warehouse and his home as an office. Russell worked from six in the morning until ten at night. This paid off and possibly because of his total commitment to the business, the company achieved rapid sales. In 1982, Russ Berrie & Co. was recognised by business magazine *Inc.* as one of the fastest growing privately owned businesses in the United States, and the company went public in 1984. Russ's soft toys are made in either Korea or China, but are made to the very highest quality and meet worldwide safety laws.

It was also during this decade that we sadly lost Princess Diana, and again the teddy bear played his part. Did you notice the sea of teddy bears, sometimes hiding among the flowers that were laid outside Buckingham Palace? By now the teddy was an emblem of lasting love and this we witnessed at the time of her death. Since her death we have also learned of her love of soft toys and teddy bears and we believe she had quite a collection. I came across a very special teddy bear who was made by Merrythought especially for Harrods. His name is Winston. He is a beautiful teddy in his own right, but he also has a tale to tell. He was bought by someone on Friday 5 September 1997, one day before the funeral of Princess Diana. He was quite obviously bought as a

A Russ Berrie bear named Glimmers.

reminder of that sad occasion because I noticed a written message on his maker's label, which is still attached to his ear, which reads: 'Diana Princess of Wales 6th September 1997. Funeral at 11.00 am at Westminster Abbey.'

Teddy bears with provenance are always highly valued by collectors. This is always worth thinking about if you are starting a collection and it is worth taking as many photographs as you can to back this up.

One teddy bear with lots of provenance is one that once belonged to Lt-Col. Bob Henderson of the Royal Scots Regiment (1904–1990). Like most other little boys, especially of those times, the young Robert Henderson loved playing soldiers with his older brother, Charles. There was great excitement in the Henderson house when a new playmate joined the boys' games, when Charles received a beautiful Steiff cinnamon bear for his birthday. Charles' brother Bob had a great fascination for the bear, who they named Teddy Boy, and to Bob's great delight Charles gifted the bear to him. A lifelong friendship between a man and his bear was born. Robert joined the military as a small firearms expert in the Royal Scots Regiment and finally was Montgomery's right-hand man during the Second World War. This did nothing to lessen Bob's interest in teddy bears; in fact, a small bear could always be found in his tunic pocket. It has also been said that Teddy Boy was with him at the D-Day Landings. When his daughter was born in 1942, Teddy Boy was given to her to play with. Imagine Bob's surprise when one day Teddy Boy was dressed for dinner in a dress! From then on Teddy Boy became better known as Teddy Girl. When Bob retired from the military he then devoted his time to finding out why the teddy bear was such a popular toy, along with Paddington Bear's creator Michael Bond and the actor Peter Bull, who were all pals of Bob and arctophiles with whom he regularly corresponded.

Merrythought's Winston, who was made exclusively for the London store Harrods.

Oliver, an early English-made teddy bear, is shown here with his original owner in an image that sums up an old bear's appeal.

Bob had about 500 teddy bears living with him at his home in Edinburgh when Teddy Girl came back to live with him, and whenever he travelled she was always there by his side. It was on Monday 5 December 1994 that I was lucky enough to be at Christie's Auction House in South Kensington, London, and had the great honour of meeting the wonderful teddy bear known as Teddy Girl, who I had heard so much about and who I waited so long to meet. In the catalogue she was described as: 'A Steiff cinnamon coloured, centre seam teddy bear, with thick curly mohair, black boot button eyes, pronounced clipped snout, black stitched nose, mouth and claws, swivel head, elongated jointed shaped limbs, shaped paws, large 'spoon' shaped feet and hump. Circa 1904 and 18 inches tall. Estimate £6,000–8,000.' She was Lot Number 32. When her lot came up, the room went quiet, as the grand old teddy was held up high for potential bidders to see. The atmosphere was electric when the bids started to come in thick and fast and there were more than just a few tears shed in that room when the hammer finally went down at £110,000. Teddy Girl now lives in a museum in Japan. Once again manufacturers were quick to pick up on this story and produce their versions of the fabulous Teddy Girl, including her makers Steiff, who not only produced a Teddy Girl, but also a Teddy Boy.

During this decade, people from just about all walks of life were now openly admitting their love for teddy bears, especially when old bears started to make enormous amounts of money when they came up for sale at auction. Teddy bear museums also started appearing, not only around Europe, but also in the United States, and indeed worldwide. The teddy bear was now definitely a talking point.

Steiff Teddy Girl.

Steiff Teddy Boy.

Alistair is an old Chiltern panda from the 1950s.

A very well-loved old Chad Valley bear named Moke with his maker's label on his foot.

Above: Two Deans Rag Book Company bears, Nigel (the smaller) and Danny.

Left: Always earning their keep; two teddies used for promotional work.

Above: A Steiff limited edition bear named Kapitan.

Right: People of all ages now admit to their love of teddy bears; they are no longer just a child's toy (shown here is an old Merrythought bear named John Silver).

During the eighties it seemed that everywhere you went collector's teddy bears, limited edition teddy bears and artist bears were looking back at you. Specialist shops opened all over the country, and they could even be spotted in local garden centres. Teddy bear fairs and shows took place, and bigger manufacturers began teddy bear clubs, including Deans. These clubs made collector's teddy bears, usually once a year, that only their club members could buy. These were usually accompanied by magazines, giving members details of the very latest bears for sale and also kept members up to date with the latest teddy bear news.

Advertisers never stopped using the teddy bear, but during the 1980s onwards his publicity potential seemed to grow even more. For example, the Cheltenham & Gloucester Building Society used Paddington Bear to encourage children to save. The Society produced very well thought out Paddington money boxes that were made of hard plastic and wore removable hats (just like the real Paddington). It is no wonder that these are highly collectable by lovers of Paddington Bear today.

The teddy bear had now come to a point in his life where he could take on his own character. He could now be whoever and whatever he wanted to be.

Girl bears were now far more acceptable than they had probably ever been, which does lead us to the question – why are teddy bears nearly always boys? I have asked this question many times and what seems to be the most common answer among teddy bear lovers and collectors is that teddy was always a friend to the doll, and so we get a girl and a boy. This, I suppose, seems fair enough.

Limited edition Merrythought bears named William and Lucky, characters that were originally created by artist John Clayton.

Limited edition Steiff 'Hot Water Bottle' bears named Otto and Warmley.

A Steiff musical bear who plays 'The Anniversary Waltz'. He was made exclusively for Harrods.

Left: Nigel, one of Deans' most iconic bears.

Below: A Steiff 'Club' teddy bear made exclusively for a New York store event in 2007.

Right: A Deans bear that was produced exclusively for a teddy bear event held at Cardiff Town Hall.

Below: A 'hug' of Deans membership bears. A new bear was produced for members annually.

Paddington Bear money boxes, which were made for promotional work.

Eric.

Captain Smith, a Hermann Spielwarren bear.

Cider, a Merrythought bear, and an old Deans doll named Betty. In days gone by, teddy was usually known as a friend to doll.

Finally

I do understand that sometimes, as we grow up, our teddy bears get lost in a world where things have changed; grown up matters take over our lives and, because of this, our teddy sometimes has to be stored away.

If you do have to do this, please show him some care and respect so that he will survive. All teddy bears become fragile and will undoubtedly deteriorate rapidly if they are exposed to dust, direct sunlight and insects. Please don't pack teddy bears away in a plastic bag, as they build up moisture, which encourages mould. Cotton bags or cardboard boxes are a much better option. Before he goes away, wrap him up in some acid-free tissue paper and then put him in a bag or box, preferably with some lavender, cloves or some cedar-wood shavings (to help prevent insect destruction). Store him in a damp-free and dust-free environment that does not suffer from extreme temperatures (like loft space).

Eileen's Bear.

The author and publisher would like to thank the following people/organisations for permission to use copyright material in this book: Margarete Steiff GmbH for images of Margarete and Richard Steiff; Fairlynch Museum, Devon, for *Cecil's Story*; Paul Hitchings Photographer for supplying studio images; and Ginosbears.co.uk for supplying many of the old bears used in this book.

Every attempt has been made to seek permission for copyright material used in this book. However, if we have inadvertently used copyright material without permission/acknowledgement we apologise and we will make the necessary correction at the first opportunity.

'Tread lightly, lest you rouse a sleeping bear'

– Soame Jenyns

Since his birth in 1902 the teddy bear has captured the hearts of young and old alike. He has survived revolutions, flown in jet fighters and taken part in land and water speed records and in times of great conflict he has stayed by his companion's side. Children everywhere adore him because he is patient with them and his universal appeal has inspired adult collectors from all over the globe to spend countless amounts of money.

With a range of previously unpublished images, teddy bear historian and collector Lorraine Hitchings offers a wonderfully nostalgic look back at one of the true icons of the twentieth century.

ISBN 9781445680491